Mouthguard

Sadie
Dupuis

Mouthguard

Gramma Press

For Dad —

I finally did the book. I'm so happy
it shares a birthday with you.

Mouthguard
Sadie Dupuis

ISBN: 978-0-9987362-8-0
First Printing

Published by Gramma Press
gramma.press
Distributed by Small Press Distribution
spdbooks.org

Cover Image: 'Companion' © 2011 Pae White
Cover Photograph: Melissa Kagerer
Book Design: Michael Heck

49 | King Chooser Has Come

In Order to Skin a Goat You Begin

I was inspired to cut it open for you.
And legs folded, it is comforting
to be able to hold to a silent time.

It is comforting to be able to hold on
by what you skin by definition.
I was inspired too. I was a blank face.

The kind where the face twists terribly.
You feel so. That is why plants look strong
in the moonlight. They choose a goat.

Me and Every Color

Strangely my interest in rainbows proved I am bad.
Revealing the rainbow's ending made everyone more curious
from where the bow sprang. I don't think about origins,
the semaphore by which one color shoots the other colors.
I only came to ruin beauty's eggy face.

Salt Circle

There's a good salon I get eyelashes
glued there an inch from my birth eyes.
The lashes I got, they shine right when damp
so I go in the pond with you.
In some cases—plenty—you lose.
Out on the grass and on trees
you didn't go inside the real one
and you never were.
Some people like mysteries
but only once they solve them
I guess it's like doing a good deed
and printing it in the newspaper.
I'm not obsessed by dying only
I already got underwater and wet.
I like the bare truthless cavities
but I don't want to test out my eyes there
like a star kicks away from its five points.
It bruises and burns to the dirt
to the sphere in the dirt which I drew there.

Saturday Bulls

Oh my heart on the cobblestone.
Some people in this world are mated
and mate themselves into a dark wall.
It is so disgusting.

Collecting the bulls, that's what they do.
They make me mated too.
Asleep they get effects like dead
or the too-big, also dead, baffling moons.

Magic isn't real, but it is so hard
to think of a bull and not expect a bull.
To not expect a bull to sprout spine
between its horn and brother horn.

Sprouted into a night corner
I burned the moon of all its impressions.
It is this kind of world.

Or it is this kind of world:
Kill yourself or kill yourself.
You suffer the same love.

Introduction

I wake up every day.
I make a list of everything I vanquish.
Now I have said more about love you.
So clumsy I am for a love you.

But my tongue makes it more "of you."
Your name is unlike mine.
I say it as much as I can.
I wake up to your divisions.

Man It Is Hard to Put Dogs in Machines

I am not like you waiting around.
I wade around in different wets.

But the lines in my skull flicker on
when I love my master's voice.

The same way his brain starts to glow
when he chooses among the girls' names.

They are Sophie and Stella and Sue
and I watch his tongue glow at the names which it made.

Still I hear names as grey and I see them as grey
same-same pointless grey spitting in pointless space.

A name as if we don't all shit from our guts.
As if shit's neither destined for maggots nor moonlight.

So I smell the moon's haze
and am blind on occasion, totally blind.

The Shadow on the Moon

Because rabbits die at sea I cannot say the name of them. They need what a fire needs and what I need. Their fur too wet to float they sink to the bottom of painted rocks. They do better in the terrifying woods. On the other hand, I'm living in a comfortable bed. I have to say I feel the rabbit head and empty in the beginning of the month. They make jumps and expect me to jump after. I have never even studied them closely. I have never put my face very close to anything and looked. There are woods from which even I am excluded.

Forests are scarier. Though its glow is heavy and I act bizarre. Though you can but do not walk the stairs or knock it with a stone. But I need no moon in the absolute night. In which the animals are enhanced. A rabbit casts his shadow on the moon and he still cannot die there. You can die in a place you can visit. With so many exclusions is it worth pretending that life is not pretend. So it is the dream of a rabbit that washes ashore. And when I go to the woods this is only my shadow.

F·R·I·E·N·D·S

My friends let me out
this way. My friends
who always say something
is the same as some other
thing the original thing is
actually unlike. Like

    real love is
plexiglass in mattress.
Or conversation
knife on a multi-tool.
Or better still heartache
sweet ass on the floor.

What do you mean my friends
who cannot contract.

         You're
making me so patient but only
so so. If you stretch your mouths
will it hold the laughs
you mouth, etc.

    My friends who
think about an in in which
they could've something something.
How that shiner redoes. How
my XXX weighs a ton.

       Oh it is
like it is they say. My friends
for whom is is.

Are You Kids Feeling in There

Tooth after tooth drumming out the more black
holes I swallow. Should know not to speak up
on empties. Mouth agag. Troughs of less color
than hyacinths pinked and forgot. Oh now I feel

wayside.
I always feel wayside
in pits of pink
forgetting
how eternity troughs
when you feel,
too.

Washing back all things
time and spittle
in a little paper cup.

I Don't Even Like Candy

Never having lived in a zoo I insist
this feels like nursing a surrogate
after my cub has perished.

Like getting sunlight
from an overhead bulb.

Oh there are people who survive
the tearing of their limb
on impact, I feel it.

I feel the impact
here
in the candy aisle.

Days and Days

I found myself just buying the situation.
Then there was some other part I act, do.

Worst house of my life and was given wrong.
Reserved and refused it was the wrong mister.

As entry to room I paid for two, and he
awarded me the changed key.

I who detain gold, who tried to refill
though I explained my rewards entitle me

to a nice place. Would you not restore
no superior correction. If all were made aware

I was awoken to looking a crack in the uncracked
and was looking through God, immediately gauche.

What Do You Want Today

For the same reason I mess up
with you in the cornmaze
let me reveal my entire hazy childhood.

I got stuck in a muddy hole.
Not much else.
Still I teach you myself.

I grab your finger
with three of my fingers
though my hands are not small.

Chariot

I direct the chariot
pulled by sphinxes.

You notice when I do something sweet
having solved the world's riddles.

Do the snakes do it like you do.
Writhe out of themselves.

You smell terrible and I love you
because I can smell you at all.

Move in with Me

And my underwater sculptures
made out of brain
the cold of the blue ocean.

A blue that doesn't mean nothing
or sadness, the way light
doesn't mean anything either.

What is a face good for anymore
if it isn't nice. It just dissolves.
Barely any face belongs.

Skeletons, crayon rubbings of them
the eels do their worst.
I have some you, they must make way.

You could live anywhere.
This is your path of shells.

We're Getting Married

It's a little like skinning. We met extremely.
It was all over, was it.
We met after not meeting, it already was.

I yanked my kidhood out of the past.
We examined what grows hooves and claws.
We had ground down our own
and had none, a kind of vow.

We marked each other up our skins.
For some time I sat on this secret.
What is love else looking back at marks.

Country Song

A handsome person I knew was now
The item of a handsome bone
That's okay
I always felt hideous in front of bone

So I went home permanently
Drank all this chocolate milk
Had a regular time
And it normally rained outside

On TV I watched the sparkle shit she sang about
I felt shame about these plain things
I do and how I dress them up
And watch myself dressing

I felt I was nothing
To celebrate

Having nothing
I wouldn't frame my day
Or make a presentation
Of my bones

I would set up half a puzzle
Then break it on the floor

I Hope Someone is Filming

Play me another sad one. I can no longer hear
the onions growing out of their carbon skins.
I can't even hear croons
rooted below the hilly carpet.

We're gonna die on this thing.
This damn thing is all rocks
sticking in my feet.

How am I moved
by the dirt on your cheeks?
I sew pockets
on your backpack and fill
these pockets with rocks.

Sinking in water
like everyday people
we get cold and wet.

I Have Never Met
a Person

Only to talk to stars it is hurtful, stars over a mountain at that.
My throat becomes a fool shouting at you stars up there.

I have seen the guts of a star sometimes
if I knew someone we'd see together.

(What I ask is for you to come down.)

A warning word I wouldn't mouth.
To hear back from the sky a word I've never seen in lights.

What I ask: for you to come down.
Show me the green guts of a star.

Ankle Bleeding
Makes the Trail

I.

I was destroying a piano with your entire body and the neighbor
kids laughed to see you fall through the keys. There was a salt line
they wouldn't cross and photos they wouldn't take. Instead
they peered through the spiral black and white books, bold
and grainy, some ground and dried herbs hardened and stacked
like every star superimposed atop every other star. The tops
of bombs all abloom. I gutted the piano's strings and buried them
under the marigolds, which are on my own side of my own fence
I forgot I had. They poked out the ground also blooming. At once
dusted you set to kniving weeds. When I am carried faster
than I can walk there is with certainty something exploding.

II.

I don't know a thing about destruction but I haven't learned much
about anything I call thing. Cars get upside down and cars
can get really burnt. Cars hang and drop from cranes in the sky.
Cop cars, keep your distance in the murderous dark.
Down along the dark road, cars upside down or in rivers.
What I mean is they get stuck in the water and time only needs
one accomplice to destroy. The way rust also overtakes string.
I find myself very ignorant, making superficial piles,
and I call myself the sorceress. No one calls me out on that.
They must not know a thing either.

III.

Flat skimming rocks in a blue topped jar which produce
the extreme bang. Like I said I don't know anything
but you look at me with huge jar eyes wondering about creating.
Watch out cops, I'm writing letters at will. I've got my undersea
glory all flipper legs and trumpets. If I've got it you've got it.
Like I got my sorcery acid painting. I compose and I break in
this floating world in the middle of a big destroy. I took a portrait
of you and me like that. We were looking in the mirror
and I stood in front of the mirror's crack. It split my face
and it felt more honest. The French in me likes smashing or spitting.
The kid in you kisses a model train. I get slouchy. I burn the next mirror.

IV.

Cloud and pixel drip into a perfect bottle spiral. You talk about
things that scared you as a kid and I've always been partial to the phrase
"the woods at night." And also partial to the woods at night.
This fear was about death and art or some shit.
Or saying why you like such and such over such and such instead
of just saying these woods at night are terrible.
Some things are so terribly mundane it is terrible
to think you are destroying yourself getting so totally normal. Like
I buy all these normal clothes on the internet which don't fit
only to bleed right into them. I read the most obvious morning newspapers.
I hear the morning rain is frightening too.
I put my head on any heart that frightens you.

V.

I know my own city and am helpless in elsewhere's
massive tunnels, it is why I ripped all the ankles I carried.
No I don't think I have a city. I lay my head on a number of things
while other people get their very heads cut through.
It is not that way with me. More a shave and a rinse.
You walk circles at your slow pace and when you back upon the
start of your blood you know you finally know you, don't you.
That's what it's like writing you these orange letters.

I put a ghost in a radio. And I would learn how certainly to make
something destroyed. But it's all car skids and burnt rock pictures.
So I wait here for the flight simulation to explode by your hands.

Erasing the Lines

thinking out for two people
and one is my partner

we are trying to break our ick
and after dropping out have lived
unimportantly the past 3 years

we are freelance real
in a community-run sound
we're a great needs recordist

now they want a friend of us

we turned and now have to show
our hideous real drivers instead
of the attractive rural bits

some enjoyment I can think
of off the top of my head

or other feedbacky delights
from my century hit list

you are desperate to work for free
and find in the annals
a place in the palm
in the phantom wrinkles of a palm

You Come Around

Grow up before becoming a cave.
Before becoming a place where intruders whisper.
Speak a language like marbles on the tongue.

How about mind ease. Flirting a self-promotion.
And no talk so also the promise of a clean future.
Moving our arms in a ridiculous daisy sway.

They say it is annoying
to protrude through the mud and rock.
Grow up before.

Unthinkable fact of entrance.
All past entrances forget.
I felt like neither nor.

When I am told the walls are solid walls I solidify.
When I remember disease in the world I dissolve rock.

Speak honestly one time.
Could you bring it out.
When I come, was I just done?

There is a way to get killed by memory.
My story so long.
Give me a minute. You do it a lot.

King Chooser Has Come

I.

Do everything everyone. The list
of figurative ghosts (the list of true ghosts)
is shrinking (is growing). A usual fever
turned unusual and again I saw
the face that saw the face of death.
He left the house of death the bicycle
cop in the parking lot. Sirens off
I know he's dead. I see door habits I know
he's dead. On the TV in the background
a man is stabbed in the ear to carols.

Past the airport along the river by the swamp
up to the church in the storm through the cemetery
I ride my bike. I ride my bike I ride the circumference
I imagine the people behind the lights (the people below
the dirt). In the back of a restaurant puking my pills
I think death has followed me to Northampton. In boxes
and stains and things taking up a new space in this plane
ticket I know he's followed me. I ask about Christmas
and if it means something. From up the winding
metal stairs I see the shade of the cemetery miles out. Him
undoing a chain. Him and his stains. I woke up not dead.

II.

From the list of his burial cities what I'll do
with my secret dirt: on his porch first morning dirt (I can't come
back to Northampton he said) (this spell
to make him move). A moonless shake tossed fresh
harms his undertaking. If he loved me dust in his boots
the sweat rising up in his feet he can stay buried. He doesn't
love me I don't love.

Go next to my father's cemetery he teased
me thinking I wouldn't. Is it a good one my lips bit.
I think so (this on the phone, his lips jutting);
I think his grave is the best one.

The flatland took dynamite to birth and now. Femur
wolf white and shells I went on the dirt, the same
pink I kissed off his nervous chest. His father's
dirt I tread. This rock uncarved his spine stiff.
Is he so rocklike.
Is he the dead.

I left Northampton I am where I live now
he buries when I try to unbury.
His ghost and my flesh unbury, his flesh and my ghost bones buried.

No not the best grave. It is his father's, let me unbury it.

III.

Have you ever had a witch?
He didn't believe in those old ghost towns
and said so. Now he isn't my only accomplice.
His muscles, they aren't in the usual
muscle spots. The King is a kind king
and rapes not. Now in the rain and on foot
it is my own salve I am refusing.

Coins and resins count the how manys and fallen
strands. Many coins to bury for my king.
Many cupboards to hide hair. You can blow
into the bloodbark. You can swill my bone
with your overtones. Dear pigs and their glass
bottles all bloodying the hooves. Pig,
you pig 'neath the moon. Pig, I'm spellmongering,
to truly have, as swine and blood and hair,
to have a spine to have.

Have you now had this witch as she would have you?
A southern man lay silvery chains about and had
and had. You pigs live just a silk decade.
The hair maggots first.
This witch, here now.

IV.

Behind the holly brush a false start for morning concussions.
Foul fate. Cracking of knightstone from the head.

I wait in our zone of concubines, brushed and sopping
up gristle stew. And you, from hitchhikers, send your valentines:

teeth excised and crusted with oak pollen, those motherfucking
oak blossoms, shed skin indigoed into a change key. Dead

trinkets. You give me the deadest. A whole autumn we deaden
beside our photorealistic tombstones. Playgrounds rust.

They build plastic ones. Boxcar killers fairytale into
campfire coal. People kill elsewhere. You grab my gristle

spots, which are gristlier. I have a body now which is now
all mine. My holly getting old and dead. You king can do

what you please with a dead body. Your dominion of holly.
They say the king only kills what he loves.

V.

Blood blistering, the skin opens
and makes no squeal. I am there
in his silent palace, slimy and cold.
His clouds don't leak. The legs
of his clock tread dancery as time
sleeps. There is slime in me now.
There is so much slime moulding
in my gut and frothing from my
mouth that I cannot say why I
need this king at all. Why I need
this slime. No more kings.

He spells his name
as his father named him.

He spells it with an x.

Milk Is Huge

Quit being sad with your piece in a mouth
like singing the same note over a shifting floor.
How it's going I just assume we all wanna die
so why bother talk. Check the levels—and—I try
to visualize white sound.

These days of nothing I go around the town
as scarecrow. Not feeling an American person
they wonder what I do inside the house.

They take something sweet; they turn it against itself.
They tell me I am too bland. So I do secret things and reveal them
blandly. Like the cream fat swimming to the mouth at the jar.

Look close, I am horrible.
I'm horrible too. I take in a cat
and he laps the large pool up.

Do You Even Remember Your Own Brain

It isn't always warm in a season
you imagine. You don't often
see the Carolinas in snow.
Frost on the ground; a scalpel. Suddenly
there is no reason to not wear it.
It's like why do you do the things you do.
Does anything really hurt or swell.
Is it only cold and tiresome because
your head doesn't want you doing
this alone. With every many mile
vague sloughing. No one remembers
the logic behind walking. Some skin
on the turf. Some skin. It's thick
and you remember
another automatic time
when legs ran because what else
but leaving.

Sarah Charles

My friend very recently was found.
Us with almost the same middle name.

Similarly there have been other deaths
a thickened heart worse in snow

in his sleep on a carpet in a car a girl
so I took out all my eyebrows.

On the phone Mom says funny depression
is only obvious when you are no longer depressed.

No I think it is always obvious,
so many brothers I could have had.

She wears big shirts to burrow in her sadness.

This Message Is for Sadie

Who is looking slash feeling
And never remotely understands
Messages she leaves herself

It's raining so the town
The whole thing is falling down
I can't get the things
I don't want to talk about

Still I love my dog and sometimes
He doesn't leave the bed either
It isn't our job
To tell you about the horror

You Can Call Me Sally

Is this god in sneakers and what kind of god
lets toplessness occur in the very first scene.

I give up on the pyramids
flowers a pig roots through
or what any animal means.

Leaf leather, skin leather,
how a little mealworm becomes
like a peacock,
the natural blues of a peacock.

My toes are the toes
of a shut-in, they can rip
through metal.

The natural sheen of car metal,
metal pins, a backbrace,
these metal hands in prayer
and fingernails, metal,

growing,
growing,

Gloss Unit

We scatter the flowers' ashes in it
what of the fish who eat them.
The one child lost a reflection.

Dry rot, a basin pool
a vacuum of the season
cannot we suck out of ourselves.

Or even magnet the stars
this pool we can't see ends in it.

Why educate the quiet ones
keep them scrumming in their dry beds.

And the bright flowers that grow
out of the soil they are starlike
and make us sorry to be grieving.

Hot Heat

That river ran faster with my bandages
dipped in it. Bandages sucked
into whirly water they unraveled.

Where white bandages once spanned
my sternum I am learning to dry
in the shade of hollow pyramids.

Could've built a very pretty curse
if I had salt in my bones. I lay down
by the bank. It didn't look so deep.

I am learning to sleep without any
bandages for the first time in my
million billion years.

When I Was Younger I Was Young

And that is why animals fight.
Their eyes under their eyes totally red.
Under their eyes in themselves they go.

An animal put under a blanket, it curves
like when it was warm… young…
It's gone from the animal that made it.

In its mind a heat, the old motion.
Why, it is glued inside of its eyes.
When I am scared the house blankets me.

Your Legs Look Alright to You

You must not believe in ghosts
because you are unkind to us.
And some time we all get dead
return to crack things open.

We don't believe you ever
tongued your rubies synthetically.

Now we frighten you
with loose parts
and our unslow revenge.

Your trivial pulse, this world
is not your world.
Misting beneath floorboards
we mustn't believe in you.

Like a victim alone in a house
like someone is in the house.
The call is coming from inside.

The Night If Any to Get Abducted

Copper exploding in neon stains
on pale nighttime
that wasn't an exaggeration.

You think I exaggerate
when dust hushes I say
in circles in air
anything about anyone's birthday party.

The boy you're my
blood brother why you
even became.

For you to drive home
moon over the milk minders
summary of groundwater
just show up and it happens.

And what came from the sky
some odd carvings.

Kicking in thoughts
like a firefly skull
what I had was
many lights and real heat.

Build a Better Do It

I

come say i am addicted to your absence here i specifically want to
joint with your lack this morning i witnessed your disappearing
membrane so i mapped where it isn't

II

i see the slow game of a dog's lifetime and see you say you'll
understand
2 bits of food and at 3 pm i despise dearness though i say it dearly

III

flexing names in my ribbed throat i just snoozed in the liner notes
more info as i wind up flinging more dearness at your grey and
great wind

IV

on the cut stone square you tell it's from a lone noose wagging its
tail in
                    the wind
cut down like any good dog it curls up shellcastlelike in a curl
submissive

V

the valley best in the pouring sun choose the pacific but my hands
are here a lot of my road mates only have a hole can we go
i want to be sitting in caves some things you droid people do i do
can we
                    go c'mon

VI

my head very close i find my head very far like a mistake magnet
and your
                    fake aura
became volatilizing water in the white morning
in the white morning sun this water corroding and the sun shouts
ripples

VII

do you have a pen draw four self-portraits compose seven
                to-do lists
sometimes a dog becomes so warm at your feet you sleep through
                your several selves

VIII

come say hey when one self ten easy ways to make sure
                just had a lot about that
talking about self for another round of summer in this blank
                season

IX

anything that's water is liars i want to ask
your water work about our disagreement here in the shadow cut
melodies of a changed line it's rainy and i've already so much to
                drive i ask the water whatever i like

X

or are you red onion layer and get your cosmic in a bottle
a comic strip of queues forever and ever wind
                    jumprope uncertainties

XI

it grows hair so can anyone find me strangle combined
to build a better do it
when the world prints these clear sheets in nature why isn't more
about
                    you transparent

XII
investigating the white blinding light of the jukebox warmed in my
interest in the scheme of now
is helter skelter the gods of anything i know

XIII
last chance to join a cadence of seasonal chews
today was you talking about today and the skeletons that make it

Mouthguard

Sometimes people ask
what it's like inside this age
I am very qualified
to discuss myself
in my wrongness
if personal mythology
is interesting to anyone

Of course I get scared out there
and at that same age I found you
I wrote my world around you
and got teeth every night
all of them silver

I chewed through
my memories of you

The yous of every city

First Date

People like to put Chicago in art
it is very big and the buildings odd
they like art-ugly faces.

You let me fall asleep
and drove my car.
I only want someone
to want me in my ugliness.

Everyone Loves an Aflame Person

It's selfish to immolate in the middle
of a funeral procession, as no one

can mourn what's cold in the coffin
with a live one on fire. Now you take

off your glasses now. They were good
for magnifying words in the clear

light of our mutual injury.
But of what use in the dark.

Everything I Know About Them

Isn't much. Is one thing. Is not to join them.
Them is sometimes slow and not all good.

Them is rare. Them is dead. Them is peering
into water. Them is on the surface longing.

Is not a myth that fills over the top and stays.
Like sleeping next to someone very sick.

Can't call them them.
Them is to abuse them. Them is separate

from the other. In them tension their only
pleasure. Is too. Them is going to break.

Who Cares About the Weatherman

Now that this winter has said screw off
the leeches return to their veins

The dirty ice melts into dirtier water
the lesser animals are feasted upon

It wasn't always such a mood
I kept in springtime or at least

I said I liked the feasting
coaxed from woods and pools

I still want you sad winter

Greenish rhododendrons
This winter was such

Go outside if you want
and take the stupid hike

it's a beautiful day out there

Will I make good use of it

The Hanged Man

I can do and do rise from the water
am forked in scarlet water
and damp vines. And I want

a hanged man, his complex of salt and sulphur
him gold and him pure.
I have not his sulphur, I wish it mine.

Oh his palms weigh down
extinguished, let me burn his bones.
I sing water songs to further stamp

his dead self one self. Now I sense
I am a half self.
Swaying, he sways, he is abundance.

With paste of his bone burnings mix my spit.
I can do and did from the water, its goldness.
Now all is all gold.

Will

To everyone who believed in me
how come. I compensate
for the world, its vast weeping.

Every time a wind comes I learn
from my ears. I owned
many things and am psychotic.

To everyone I leave everything
intangible, someone ought
to care about those things.

Pawning off coppery anger
in the fall anymore. No longer
I wish to make this stuff up.

You Looked So Pretty This Morning

I was being the dark hill when it awed
itself. Its staunch confrontation
with heaven's can crushing. Its stubble

and scales
and roadfat

in a machete moonlight glittering.
No two come on each other
like it came on itself when it did.

No two souping along
with trees in the roadmiddle burning
slow and slow.

Who built the road of all these things.

The road I was when pavement.
Horses and semen and sudokus
I screwed up in the road.

Slower I was being concrete and slower.

Storms

We stormed in every position
the snow like caking soap
crunched and balled

At calendar speed
the winds walled

At mammoth speed
on old wood porches
the whiting stoop toppled

And roofs collapsed and mirrors
frosted as they could not bear
our storm eyes

We are going to die someday
and better not be obsessed

The Vermonter

I put hands on its steel
it fussed in place
hardened my fingers
it stormed metallic
over the bridge the water
frozen purple you too ran
along the moon and we loved
each other and the people inside
they felt their own hands

It is not my train
but I wait for it at night
and am stubborned by its sandmass
when I did flesh out
supine on the tracks
the nettle-dredged going train gored and grabbed
oh for you I destroy
all trains and ride every

Hounds halloo
bark back trains
in the dim morning
do I then fear you
never may dismount
these tracks unfold
and very bullish
I pad after trains panting after
people on whichever train
to wherever I love you
on the train staring out

at the windowed woods
the fragile moony ice
the lake water tainted is not my lake
the autumn lake of disconnect
thank you you left me
behind with love

Acknowledgments

To my teachers Dara Wier, Peter Gizzi, Saskia Hamilton, Timothy Donnelly, Jed Berry, and Josh Bell, for seeing something in my work, and for tolerating me in your workshops.

As well as my teachers James Tate, Rebecca Faery, and Bill Corbett (who I blame for my life as a poet). Their guidance was vital, especially when we disagreed, and they are very missed.

Thank you to the Program for Poets & Writers at UMass-Amherst for introducing me to so many writers who've become my favorites, and for giving me three whole years to bike around and think up this sad, weird book. And of course to the writing departments at Barnard and MIT.

Thank you to *Sixth Finch*, *Everyday Genius*, and *ILK Journal* for publishing earlier versions of some of these poems, and to ODE for printing a broadside of "Saturday Bulls."

Colleen Louise Barry turned my "would it be totally annoying if i sent you a manuscript sometime?" cold email into a real-ass book. Thank you to her and everyone else at Gramma Press, particularly Aidan Fitzgerald, Danniel Schoonebeek, and Michael Heck, for your impressive work at transforming a doc in the cloud into the real-ass thing this reader is now holding. Not to mention Alex Kadvan, Marisa Brown, and everyone at Brilliant Corners for their co-conspiratorial help in the plotting.

Thank you to my friends who pried poems out of me/traded writing back/ coaxed me into reading in public (even though it freaks me out). Especially, but not limited to: Michael DeForge, Melissa Broder, Ted Powers, Wendy Xu, Joshua Jennifer Espinoza, Brian Foley, Brandon Stosuy, Dorothea Lasky, Dylan Baldi, Caroline Crew, Sam Rosenberg, Melissa Lozada-Oliva, Mark Leidner, and Mira Gonzalez.

And especially thanks to Diane Dupuis, my mom, who was of course the first person to convince me I might be a writer.

Photo by Katrina Barber

Born in New York, NY in 1988, Sadie Dupuis is the guitarist, vocalist and songwriter
for the rock band Speedy Ortiz, and the producer and multi-instrumentalist behind
politically-geared pop outfit Sad13. She holds an MFA from UMass Amherst, and
has written cultural criticism for outlets including *Nylon*, *Playboy*, and *Spin*.
Based in Philadelphia, PA, this is her first book of poetry.